Developing F
Practice for Preachers

Charles Chadwick
Vicar of Bridgwater St Mary and
Chilton Trinity and Durleigh

Phillip Tovey
Training Officer
Diocese of Oxford

14/2/05

*A day of present-giving on Valentine's Day.
May the spirit flow between us for
many more years to come; I know the
teachings of leadership will have borne fruit.*

GROVE BOOKS LIMITED
RIDLEY HALL RD CAMBRIDGE CB3 9HU

With much love,

alex

Contents

Acknowledgements

We would like to thank Rev John Waller who started to work on this book with Phillip but then had to give up, and graciously allowed Charles to take over his place. We would also like to thank members of the congregation at Saint Peter and Saint Paul, Stokenchurch for their help in data collecting, various groups of people in ministry in the Diocese of Oxford, and members of the Group for the Renewal of Worship. In particular we thank David, Anne, John, Julia and Ian for their stories. Thanks also goes to Rev Chris Byworth, Rev John Leach, and Rev Ian Tarrant for their detailed feedback on an earlier version of the text. Finally we thank Tricia Chadwick for her helpful proof reading.

The Cover Illustration is by Peter Ashton

First Impression June 2001
ISSN 0144-1728
ISBN 1 85174 466 5

1
Learning Our Stories

The gospel...creates the true preacher and the true sermon.[1]

We have been friends for more than twelve years. We have both been parish ministers and kept in contact to talk informally about work. Over recent years our ministries have had a particular emphasis on adult teaching and learning. Charles' time with an ecumenical training programme led him to think further about how people learn. Phillip took a diocesan training post. Thus we have both become interested in learning from experience. We each experienced a significant event related to preaching and will begin by telling these particular stories.

Phillip's Story

My job entails me regularly organizing a day workshop on introduction to preaching. While I sought ideas for how best to deliver this teaching, a significant conversation happened. In a group discussing preaching one person said that many ministers do some initial training in preaching and then stop thinking about it. They just do it for years and they never reflect on their practice. As the discussion proceeded I became more and more uncomfortable. I realized that I had not looked at a book on preaching since my curacy, seven years before. I had adjusted my preaching as I had moved parishes twice, but not done any significant review. In fact I thought I was a pretty good preacher. Now I began to think that I had not been very thoughtful about how I preach. I had become stuck in a rut, doing it in one particular way. This was in part because in my last parish job I preached fairly regularly three times on Sunday. The sheer volume of preaching had driven out reflection. But this was no help in teaching preaching, and I could not answer the question of what ten years of preaching had taught me. In fact I felt rather ignorant. It was one of those events that I wanted to talk over with someone.

Charles' Story

I hold regular review sessions with the lay leaders of one of the churches I serve. We consider what is going well, what is not going well, and how we might improve things. We try to look at every aspect of church life, not least how we interact with one another. At one meeting we discussed the whole topic of feedback and criticism, and we wondered why such a topic seemed difficult. To continue to function solely at the level of, 'People only say anything if they are unhappy,' seemed a little limiting, to say the least. So we began to build in a process of reflection and review of what we do as a church. This made me begin

---

1   P T Forsyth, *Positive Preaching and the Modern Mind* (London: Paternoster Press, 1907, 1998) p 9.

to question my own practices, particularly in the area of leading worship and preaching. I had always prepared and preached sermons on the basis of, 'My aim in this sermon is to inspire the congregation to...' I had never sought any structured feedback to help me consider my own style of preaching, nor had I asked people what they actually heard compared with what I thought they might be hearing. It struck me that to try and obtain people's views on my preaching could both help me to learn from their and my experience and had the potential to help us as a church in our task of being a learning community. But how might we do this?

Review

Our stories made us think that the whole topic of reviewing our preaching was of considerable importance, not least in light of the time and value the sermon is given both by preachers and congregations. At a discussion with friends, it turned out that there were some noteworthy stories of how people had changed their preaching. We discussed them and thought that these were significant in terms of learning about preaching and being a preacher. Many other stores could be added. The point of these is to view different experiences and so begin to learn more about preaching. You might begin to ask yourself about your experience and what you have learned. This booklet is not aiming to join the multitude of publications that deal with the logistics of preaching. Rather our concern is with reviewing your approach to preaching and using your experience as the basis for learning new things, and trying new approaches. To help us do this we shall draw on some more stories.

2
Hearing More Stories

Few of us are taught how to preach; for the most part we are left to teach ourselves by the clumsy and hazardous expedients of trial and error.[2]

In this chapter we continue the stories of preachers and their experience. Let us read their stories first before making any comment.

David's Story

My first sermon, as a trainee minister, was an essay on 'Treasure in Heaven.' I was a stockbroker at the time! It was based solely on my observation of Anglican clergy over my 24 years. I wrote it out and read it out, word-by-word. At theological college I was instructed in both homiletic principles, and a method: *placere—docere—movere* (to please—to teach—to move). Subsequently I refined this to include an hour in the study for every minute in the pulpit, to use only biblical illustrations, and I continued to write it all out in full.

I was influenced by Jonathan Edwards, who advocated exegesis (the exposition of a passage from the Old Testament), appropriation (the use of a New Testament passage that 'Christianized' the Old Testament passage) and improvement (the practical application of the teaching to contemporary life.) For several years I followed his lead, preaching now from extended outline notes.

In the 1980s, under the influence of charismatic renewal, although I still pursued Edwards' approach, I began from time-to-time to 'float free' from my notes, even finding myself sometimes saying things I had not even thought of before! Eventually this developed into an entirely extempore practice. Generally without any notes at all, I found myself following in the footsteps of the old black preachers of the Deep South, 'I reads meself full, I thinks meself straight, I prays meself hot, and I lets meself go!'

Now I am in a multi-parish country benefice, with up to three preachments on a Sunday morning, all at Communion, and with strict time-restraints and old-age creeping on, things have changed again. I read the lectionary readings, identify a single point, select a text and read up on it, prepare a contemporary 'parable,' which is usually a humorous personal anecdote. I quietly pray in tongues at the chancel step, and offer my pulpit prayer: 'Lord, give your word now like rain and snow, that there may be seed for the sower and bread for the eater that your word may accomplish that which you purpose, and not return to you empty; in Jesus' name.' Then it is 'parable,' text, Bible-based teaching, personal testimony, exhortation/application, and relationship to Communion, and closing prayer. And no notes!

---

2   C Smyth, *The Art of Preaching* (London: SPCK, 1940) p 2.

Anne's Story

I have preached for some ten years or more. As a lay person, without a licence to preach, most of my experience was originally in informal worship, where I was mostly addressing those fairly new to faith, those on the fringe of the church, or those who were young in years. I would prepare carefully but not write anything down, so at the point of delivery the 'sermon' appeared to be off the cuff. I almost always used something visual that required careful preparation.

Four years ago I became a Reader and subsequently was ordained. I now also preach much more formally in the main Sunday Eucharist and at Evensong. For these services my preaching style has changed completely, with the whole script being written down, even though I might deviate from it when preaching. I find this discipline hard, but think it gives me more varied and reflective material to offer the congregation, which is more mixed and less easy to predict than at informal worship.

John's Story

For two years I have been itinerant, preaching around the country in a variety of settings on the subject of charismatic renewal. Compared with being based in one congregation it is, in many ways, very different. Every sermon is a one-off. I have to work with the uncertainty of preaching in a completely unknown situation. I feel that I have about four minutes to convince people that I am worth listening to and that I have the right to stand before them. There is also the pressure of trying to achieve the best on every occasion, as people's expectations of me are high.

The content, too, is often different, as I am not preaching with the usual long-term sense of building up the body of Christ. There is also the question of repeating sermons. On the road I can use a talk many times in diverse settings. I have developed a very thorough database of what I have said where. It has been revealing to note which talks have had such merit that they can be delivered again and again and which I felt had quickly passed their sell-by date. Many things are the same, of course. I have maintained my habit of using an OHP acetate with outline points to help people follow the logic of the talk. I still expect and preach towards some kind of a response. All in all it has proved fascinating to note the changes in my style which the new role has forced on me.

Julia's Story

I have been working in the same UPA parish for eight years. From the beginning I have tried to follow the formula for sermon writing that says there should be 12 hours to prepare and write it, 12 minutes to deliver it, and 12 seconds to tear it up and throw it in the waste paper bin! I have tried to root the content of my preaching in the freshness and relevance that springs from everyday living and seeing God at the centre of the ordinary.

At one level the way in which I write, the syntax, the selection of words has altered only with the rhythm of events, shifting to fit the mood and the moment.

At another level there has been a profound change in the way I try to express things. As my ministry has evolved and matured, and as the level of trust between us has grown, so the list of shared experiences and common bonds has lengthened, while the number of weekly sermons I have delivered has mounted up. As a result my style has become simpler, more direct, perhaps starker, yet incorporating more humour than when I first came to the parish. To put it succinctly, I have moved from delivering an oil painting each week to sharing a pencil sketch.

Review

These four personal preaching histories reveal that adjusting one's preaching tends to arise for a variety of reasons. These can include changes in one's theology, receiving additional training, developments in one's ministry, preaching in different contexts, and preaching to different congregations. It is our belief that by telling your story you will gain a greater appreciation of what have been the influences on your own preaching. So what is your story? What is your personal preaching story?

3

Approaches to Learning from Preaching

The vast majority have to learn this thing [preaching]…
It is one of the dangers of the Church of England that so many don't learn it.[3]

Having read several different stories we now want to develop the issue of learning from experience. What approaches might we use to learn and grow as preachers? We can see from the stories that our preaching needs to evolve and mature. This may be in response to a number of factors. But to learn from the experience of preaching there is a prior question that needs to be addressed, and that relates to the validity of experience as a starting point.

Starting from Experience

In a revealed religion such as Christianity it may seem strange to some to ask questions from experience. Paul exhorted Timothy to 'preach the word; be prepared in season and out of season; correct, rebuke and encourage—with great patience and careful instruction' (2 Timothy 4.2). Is then not the preacher to concentrate on exegetical accuracy and godly application? Is that the end of the story? Clearly the Scriptures are about a revelation. One tradition in the Scriptures is that of the prophets who speak the word of the Lord. The Old Testament prophets could be formidable preachers, as was Jeremiah at the Temple gate (Jeremiah 7). Some have seen this as the model for the Christian preacher.[4] But this is only one approach in the Scriptures. Another strand in both the Old and New Testament is that of wisdom. The wise were able to give instruction and teaching, the book of Proverbs being one example of that teaching and Jesus' proverbs, sayings and parables being another. In this tradition a different methodology is found. Wisdom is 'The project of making a continuous whole out of one's existence.'[5] Wisdom seeks 'a fresh view of the transcendent as an ordering factor.'[6] Thus a feature of 'proverbial (experiential) wisdom' is 'to encapsulate different aspects of wise behaviour; to describe the way things are.'[7] Beginning with experience is an approach that links back to the wisdom tradition. Likewise, the issue of passing on our experience and wisdom to others who are beginning to preach has a wisdom dimension. If we begin from our experience of preaching we can ask the question: how do we learn from this experience?

Alan Mumford and Peter Honey find four approaches to 'learning from expe-

3   Canon Twells, 1889, cited in C Smyth, *The Art of Preaching* (London: SPCK, 1940) p ix.
4   See W Perkins, *The Art of Prophesying* (Edinburgh: Banner of Truth, 1996, 1606) and J R W Stott, *The Preacher's Portrait* (London: Tyndall Press, 1961).
5   See, A Winton, *The Proverbs of Jesus: Issues of History and Rhetoric* (Sheffield: JSOT Press, 1990) p 79.
6   *ibid*, p 77.
7   *ibid*, p 29.

rience at work' and have developed a classification.[8] They call these four approaches intuitive, incidental, retrospective and prospective.

The Intuitive Approach

This involves 'learning from experience, but not through a conscious process. The person using the intuitive approach claims that learning is an inevitable consequence of having experiences.'[9] This is an osmotic theory—'caught not taught.' It will lead to the ability to catalogue quite a lot of experience but not to say much about learning and development from that.

The description of Phillip's learning at the beginning of this booklet is intuitive. There was more than ten years of experience. There was a description of some changes made as he moved parishes. There was also a feeling that preaching was satisfactory—and much verbal feedback to that effect. But there was no development plan or talk of consciously taking different approaches. It appears that this approach did not equip him to pass on his wisdom, except in some very broad terms.

This might be true of many busy parish clergy. Perhaps it is not until they have to supervise someone such as a Reader in training, that they begin to reflect on their own experience and think through their own approach. It is common in busy church life to get reasonable feedback about preaching, on the lines of, 'Nice sermon, Vicar,' without taking this any further and omitting to look for ways to develop the ministry of preaching. Reviewers sometimes say that many clergy express satisfaction in their preaching ministry, but bishops often get requests for better preachers in an interregnum. There seems to be a gap in perception between preachers and congregations, to which we will return.

The Incidental Approach

This involves 'learning by chance from activities that jolt an individual into conducting a *post mortem*.'[10] This can happen for a variety of reasons, something out of the ordinary occurs, expectations are not fulfilled. Mulling over the event then happens in an informal way. Honey and Mumford stress that in this approach learning is used as an insurance, to cover your back, but conclusions are not reached.

In moving to a new post you may have to adjust your preaching. This is achieved by asking questions about what happened before. For how long are people expected to preach? Where does it come in the service? Adjustments are made because of feedback and by trial and error. Julia talked about making such adjustments in her story.

By talking to people about their experiences we have discovered other examples of incidental approaches. In light of an upcoming ministry review, Helen

---

8   A Mumford, *Effective Learning* (London: Institute of Personnel and Development, 1995). P Honey and A Mumford, *The Opportunist Learner* (Maidenhead: Peter Honey, 1995).
9   *Ibid*, p 22.
10 *Ibid*, p 22.

perceived that she could benefit from some further training. She chose to attend a Continuing Ministerial Education day on preaching. The day's quality was such that Helen felt encouraged to buy a book on preaching and read it. The CME day happened to be there and so, feeling under pressure, Helen went. What if the event was less stimulating? No challenge would have happened and Helen may have continued in her old ways without anything like a serious review.

The Retrospective Approach

This approach 'involves learning from experience by looking back over what happened and reaching conclusions about it.'[11] This can be produced as a diagram:

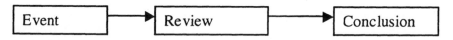

In this approach 'considered conclusions are knowingly reached.'[12]

This might be the result of going on a course or a change in approach. As a result of the good CME day Helen began to review her preaching and read some books that made her think. Gradually she began to incorporate her new insights into her practice. John's story talked of the changes involved in becoming an itinerant preacher. He came to some definite conclusions about using the sermon more than once, about the time he has to make an impression, about the subject on which he preaches. Thus he has worked himself into a different style from that used in ministering to a regular congregation. In all these changes there is a deliberate learning but this category tends to be reactive because the changes come about through change of circumstances and perceptions.

The Prospective Approach

This is the final approach of Honey and Mumford. This builds on the retrospective approach by adding planning to learn before the experience. Thus there is a proactive element to this approach to learning. The diagram then changes to:

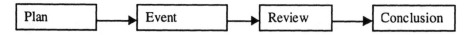

Often this can be the approach when going on a course. The need to study preaching may be as a result of a ministry review and so a course is recommended. This also happens in initial training in preaching. Jill, a Reader candidate, was aware that her delivery was weak—she had got feedback that she was rather boring. So she attended a training day on public speaking. She developed her insights from this and put them into action. Thus, Jill worked in a prospective way and dealt

---

11 Mumford, *Effective Learning*, p 23.
12 *ibid*, p 23.

with her problems. Too often after initial training, preaching is only incidentally reviewed and developed.

In one church the whole preaching team went together on a preaching weekend as a result of a review. They had questions they wanted to ask, for example, how can we deliver better expository sermons? They were then enabled to develop their preaching ministry together. The important thing here is that there was some targeting of what was wanted in the learning. This was carried through to implementation by reviewing the learning and planning to change their preaching practice.

Later we will look at the ways preaching can be reviewed; if the preachers in a church or benefice can work together their mutual evaluation can be helpful. Appropriate questions include: Am I getting into a rut? Is preaching getting worse due to lack of time for preparation? Has the preaching gradually lost connection with the congregation? A review can help lead to an identification of needs and a plan for development.

Learning from Preaching

The approaches set out above show a progression from reactive to proactive. It might well be that our preferred style is the intuitive approach to our preaching. Professional development approaches suggest that we should consider becoming more proactive. This might be in a number of areas:

- Improving our abilities in known weaknesses.
- Greater knowledge of the biblical text.
- Enhancing our delivery skills.
- Developing our theology of preaching.
- Preaching in different styles.
- Preaching on topics we have neglected.

One way for you to develop is to begin to think of your learning from preaching and to see which of the approaches you are taking. It is likely that you are intuitive most of the time. However, there may have been occasions when some feedback has stopped you short. Think about that and see what conclusions you reach. Maybe like Helen you have been on a course. Look back at what you learned and what you implemented. Consider your own story, as we suggested at the end of the last chapter, and look through the approaches to learning that you have used. Doing this now will help you to understand further the four methods and relate them to aspects of your practice. This is one way to start your development. We are going to suggest some more strategies for action in the next chapter.

4
Approaches to Reflective Practice in Preaching

Anything that encourages feedback, experimentation, disagreement, variety,
fellowship and cross-fertilization can't be bad.[13]

So far the stories of preachers have been recounted and some approaches to learning have been described. In a process of learning the next question might be, What do I do next? This chapter therefore makes a series of suggestions about ways of learning from the experience of preaching. All have been tried by others or us and found helpful. These are not necessarily discrete strategies and to some extent they overlap. It may be helpful to use a number of different approaches. The stories used in this booklet include examples of all the approaches. The exercises that follow are not ranked in any particular order, and it might be that you would find some more helpful than others. They form a set of suggestions of what might be helpful in order to learn more from your experience of preaching. All we recommend is that you try them and see.

Supervision
a) *Being supervised.* We have already noted that supervision is common when beginning to preach. At this point a more experienced preacher will give feedback to the trainee. This may involve both the preparation of the text of the sermon and its delivery. It rests on an apprenticeship model, doing it alongside. This can be one way of learning and it can be very encouraging. When this ends, we feel the confidence of a practitioner who says 'You can now do it on your own.' Once licensing or ordination has taken place, the apprenticeship tends to fade as the new preacher gains confidence. Often the feedback from other preachers or the congregation starts to dry up, but there are ways that preachers can develop feedback on their preaching.
b) *Peer supervision.* It may be possible for a team of preachers to supervise one another. In supervision there is a sense of one or more persons giving directive advice. But support and encouragement should also be a part of the process.
c) *Becoming a supervisor.* Many people find that after a number of years their role changes to supervising. This sort of training is important, and needs to be thought about carefully. It may be that someone is on a placement. It may be that a new Reader is in training. It need not be the team leader who does the supervision. Someone else in the team may be the best-gifted person for this task. There are important skills in supervising and these need to be carefully considered.[14]

---

13 David Day, *A Preaching Workbook* (London: Lynx, 1998) p vii.
14 See P Hawkins and R Shohet, *Supervision in the Helping Professions* (Buckingham: Open University, 2000).

Consultancy

a) *Working with a consultant.* Sometimes more experienced preachers are willing to spend time with someone else to help them improve their preaching. It might be that this is only a part of a work consultancy arrangement or it might be a specialized preaching consultancy.[15] This is distinct in that the consultant is an outsider and the contract is by arrangement.

b) *Becoming a consultant.* The other side of this is for more experienced and trained preachers to take on a consultancy role. This might entail being involved in every aspect of preaching—preparation, delivery and review—and thus it requires time to be available for all of these.

Feedback

a) *Peer feedback.* Anne preaches where there are a number of preachers and a ministry team. They have an ongoing process of getting feedback on preaching. A feedback sheet is given to members of the ministry team on their arrival at church and they fill it in. The preacher may also fill in the form. This then enables a contrast between self-evaluation and feedback from others. Anne says that this focuses the mind of the preacher in clarifying what the sermon is aiming to say and gives the preacher some idea of what people have heard.

In doing this it is important to build up a positively critical community. Too often in church life people are afraid to engage in feedback because there is a very negatively critical atmosphere—if you do not do it brilliantly you get told so very loudly! Linked to this there is little positive feedback and praise of what is good. A positively critical community could give both praise and encouragement as well as suggesting areas for improvement.

b) *Congregational feedback.* If you are not in a church with a number of preachers then it is possible to ask the laity to give you feedback if only by an evaluation form.[16] Charles chose to do this over a period of several weeks. A variety of laity from different ages, genders and positions in the church were asked to fill in a feedback form. This involved eight different people as two people were asked each week. In discussing the results of this Charles discerned some outcomes:

- That overall this was a very helpful process and felt good.
- That ending the sermon was important and could be improved.
- That it made Charles think more about the aim of the sermon and how the congregation saw this.
- That people noticed when, in a busy week, preparation had been skimped.
- That those who were involved said they listened harder because of what they had to do, but that this was no bad thing.

This was something that was simple to do and could easily be repeated in a few years time.

---

15 See G Lovell, *Consultancy, Ministry and Mission* (London: Burns and Oates, 2000).
16 See P Ballard and J Pritchard, *Practical Theology in Action* (London: SPCK, 1996) pp 175–176.

c) *Self evaluation*. We have already seen one method—filling in the evaluation form yourself. Another way to develop reflection on practice is to keep a preaching journal. Note down your thoughts and feeling in a notebook about a number of your sermons. After you have preached a few look back at what you have written. Are there any trends or particular issues? Can you identify things you would like to do as a part of your life-long learning?

Learning Partnerships

Another approach is to contract with someone to examine preaching as a partnership. Here you would both come together from time to time and one would share some experience while the other would ask questions that facilitate this learning. Thus the aim is to help the other explain and reflect on his or her experience rather than to offer answers. This would be a learning partnership.[17] Thus, once a month the partners could meet together and each could share the answer to the question, What have I learned about preaching since we last met? Journalling is a way to record the experience and capture it for the sharing session. Some people find that doing a SWOT analysis (strengths, weaknesses, opportunities and threats) is a helpful way to summarize their reflections.[18] Charles and Phillip contracted such a partnership for 6 months. This has resulted in an ongoing discussion about preaching, some of the fruit of which is to be found in this booklet.

Group Preparation

a) *Peer*. Some may find that they are in a ministry team. This may meet to study the Scriptures together and from this develop the themes for preaching for that week. This has been found to be a rich experience for some. Here the preparation for the sermon becomes a group exercise.

b) *Mixed*. This can also be done in a mixed group of preachers and non-preachers. A Bible study group can look at the passages for next Sunday and share their reflections on them. If preachers are part of the group then they will have some of the heart of the congregation with them when they prepare the sermon later in the week. Charles, from time to time, has made known to the congregation that he will be available on a particular time for an *ad hoc* group to meet to look at next week's lessons for a similar purpose.

Profiling

It is possible that you may be asked to use a profiling procedure to review your ministry. This happens to Readers and those involved in various portfolio schemes. In this, various criteria will be set up and an evaluation grid is created so that you can do self-evaluation. The grid in chapter seven comes from the Reader *Profiles* document.[19] This is a part of a more all-round review of ministry and the

---

17 See J Robinson, S Saberton, and V Griffin, *Learning Partnerships: Interdependent Learning in Adult Education* (Ontario: Ontario Institute of Adult Education, 1985).

18 See F and R Bee, *Facilitation Skills* (London: IPD, 1998) p 169.

19 Central Readers Council, *Profiles: A Tool for the Review of Reader Ministry* (London: CRC, 1997).

preaching section has been extracted from a larger document.

Phillip found this to be a useful start to examine and reflect on his preaching. It was fairly easy to tick boxes and so give some quick idea of strengths and weaknesses. He found it more demanding to brainstorm what the evidence might be to back this up. The profile was then used as one section for a larger preaching portfolio.

Preaching Portfolio

A portfolio is a collection of evidence that shows you can do something, know something, or have a particular skill. They are increasingly popular in formal education in practice-based subjects. They are also being recommended for ongoing training and development, for example in teaching the Booth Report suggests a 'Portfolio of Teaching Experience and Development.' It is possible to do the same thing with preaching. Evidence for the portfolio might include preparation notes, sermon notes, self-evaluation, the feedback of others. If this is all collected together from a number of sermons then there is a substantial amount of evidence. Phillip tried this out, collecting evidence over six sermons. He found:

- This showed him that his preaching had changed in recent times.
- That he was quite influenced by a recent study of experiential learning.
- That he valued preaching more than he thought he did.
- That talking it over with someone else was quite helpful to give an alternative perspective.

Wading through all the evidence is not always simple. In a voluntary partnership this is done quite quickly when one person introduces a portfolio to the other. The key piece of work is to identify points of learning from the evidence and begin to make plans for development.

Training Events and Study

A number of organizations run specific events on preaching such as Praxis, the College of Preachers and the Proclamation Trust. Dioceses may run CME days on preaching. There are many excellent courses on how to make a presentation.

While there are posts for professors of preaching in North America, there is no such thing here. However, the College of Preachers runs courses that can result in a Certificate or an MA in Preaching.[20]

There are many good books on preaching to read.[21] Some magazines, such as *The Expository Times* and *The Reader*, very much have the preacher in mind. There are increasing facilities and resources for preachers on the internet. There is of course often a North American bias in this but the range of material is expanding all the time.

---

20 See, College of Preachers, http://www3.mistral.co.uk/collpreach/index1.htm (Jan 2001).
21 See these footnotes!

Using Tools and Exercises

Another approach is to take a variety of diagnostic tools and use them to look at the sermon either before or after it has been delivered. There are a number of books which desribe such tools.[22] These of course have their own particular view of what preaching is about, which may not be yours. A few of the approaches are included in the last chapter. These could become a part of a portfolio, or might be used by others in the preaching team, or in a preaching partnership to stimulate thinking and discussion. They cover both preparation and delivery. But there will be problems if, like David, you preach without a text and you may need to tape some of your sermons. If, however, you type your sermons into the computer, these tools may have great potential for you.

Review

The aim of this chapter has been to introduce a variety of approaches to becoming reflective about our preaching. These have all been road tested and used in developing preaching. They do not cover every possibility and in some cases overlap. However, our conviction is they can be used to enrich your preaching ministry. This chapter ends like the other by encouraging you to get involved in some way. Where do you think you are? Where do you want to go? How and where might God be calling you in your ministry as a preacher? Which of the above approaches might help?

---

22 For example, A C Rueter, *Making Good Preaching Better* (Collegeville: The Liturgical Press, 1997).

5
Looking Again

Dare to look again at those preaching notes.[23]

The aim of this chapter is to both review and develop the argument of this booklet. We began with incidents that made each of us stop and think. We then went on to discuss this with others, whose stories further widened our questions and we developed from this the idea of a personal preaching story. Next we introduced a piece of theory about approaches to learning to begin to assess how we have been learning in our personal history. Then we have suggested various strategies for action. This has been a deliberate plan, starting with experience and self-evaluation and then going on from there to possible courses of action. Now we want to look back in secondary reflection, to learn more deeply and to relate the learning so far to further pieces of theory, which ties our approach together.

Kolb's Learning Cycle

In the field of experiential learning the American David Kolb has made a profound impact. His theory of the learning cycle has been adopted and adapted by many people. It has stood the test of time as an explanatory model and can be summarized in a simple diagram:[24]

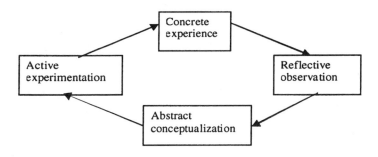

The slightly complex terminology that Kolb used can be summarized in the following cyclical diagram:

23   Donald Coggan, *New Day for Preaching* (London: SPCK, 1987, 1996) p 64.
24   D A Kolb, 'The Process of Experiential Learning,' in M Thorpe (ed), *Culture and Processes of Adult Learning* (London: Routledge, 1993).

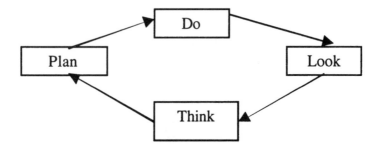

In experiential learning you can jump into the cycle at any point, but you must complete the whole cycle to show the learning. Implicit in this is that learning is about action as much as thinking—it is a process leading to change. Creating plans, developing anecdotes and knowing more theory are not necessarily learning in this model. The model challenges us to show the development of our practice and its interrelationship with theory. Historically, in the church, the model of education has been to provide learners with lots of theory and calling this learning. Kolb's model, however, asks questions about the relationships of theory with practice. As such it is a model of learning that is important both in the initial training and in the life-long learning of the ministers of the church. It is a theory that emphasizes learning as development rather than the accumulation of facts.

This model can be related to preaching in that we may get theory through books and courses, or we may have a great deal of practice. The question then becomes: what have we learned and how are we growing? Reflection on our practice is needed to answer this question and this reflection must include going on to planning and development.

From the stories in this booklet we see that learning has often been haphazard. As contexts change so people have had to learn new things. Anne had to learn some new skills once she preached at evensong. John had to adjust to an itinerant preaching ministry. David changed after a charismatic experience.

Others have been proactive in learning. Helen was inspired by the CME day and this led to a plan of study and experimentation in new ways. Charles looked for feedback, in part through a review of church life. In these stories learning is growth, where theory and practice are put together in the learning cycle.

Jill's story illustrates Kolb's cycle. Her experience was of being told her voice was boring in preaching. Reflecting on this she went off on a course of public speaking. This gave her more confidence to try and vary her pace and pitch more. She then preached when one of us was present. The feedback was, 'I can see you are working on this, keep doing it more.' This led to more confidence and greater boldness in her use of voice in preaching. Meeting one of us again she joyfully announced that folk had come up to her to say how much her preaching had improved and that now they could hear what she was saying they were much encouraged by her word. In this short story you can see a continuing spiral of action and reflection leading to the development of a preaching ministry.

Levels of Reflection

Kolb is a simple model of learning that relates action and reflection. The latter has itself a number of different levels, all of which need to be included in reflection on preaching. These can be seen as:

- The action. This is the preparation and delivery of the sermon. It may include some of the spontaneous changes made while preaching (reflection-in-action).[25] For example, in the pulpit you may begin to change what you are saying because you realize that the congregation is not whom you expected.
- The reflection. This is reviewing the action itself (reflection-on-action). What went right and wrong? How did people react? How will I change what I say and do next time? What did others think? This can be done with the variety of methods that we have suggested. This level of reflection is to look at last week's sermon and ask questions about it of yourself and others.
- Secondary reflection. This is a more reflective review of a season of preaching. How is my preaching developing? What ways have I changed my preaching? What have I been learning? Do I see needs for further learning? Are there points of encouragement? The preaching history is more important here than last week's sermon. It puts the latter in a context.[26]

This outlines reflection as a way to develop and grow in preaching. Often this will require feedback, discussion with others who preach, and developing our own learning and growth. You can be engaged in reflection in a number of ways.

- This might be in the car driving to the next service, when you are to preach the sermon again, thinking about improvements. Or it might be in the service when the congregation is not as expected. Both of us have had to adjust our preaching in these circumstances.
- You might want to review a particular sermon and see how you could improve it. If this is done sometime after the initial delivery this is reflection-on-action. We have both done this from time to time.
- If this is done after a number of years of practice, this might be a major review and it is secondary reflection. For us, writing this booklet and developing teaching courses has encouraged us to this deeper review.

We recommend you to take time to do deeper reflection.

Review

If you look back at your story can you see cycles of learning? What has caused these? Has it been a response to circumstances or something else? What we are commending in this chapter is to identify cycles of learning in your preaching story. Then ask: did doing this change your boundaries of perception or are you still working within them? We would like to suggest that this is all a part of 'rightly handling the word of truth' (2 Tim 2.15).

---

25 See D Schon, *The Reflective Practitioner* (Aldershot: Ashgate, 1983, 1991).
26 See A Brockbank and I McGill, *Facilitating Reflective Learning in Higher Education* (Buckingham: Open University Press/SRHE, 1998) pp 76–84.

6
Moving On

Scripture is not interpreted in isolation, but in dialogue with experience and perspectives of a local community of faith.[27]

It is our belief that across the church there is an increased interest in preaching. The advent of *The Times* newspaper and College of Preachers' search for examples of good practice, with their 'Preacher of the Year' award started in 1995, is a good instance of this. The weekly sermon is often the only means by which the majority of church worshippers are enabled to be led further in faith. Its value should not be underestimated.

> Real preaching, when it is heard and submitted to, can move people to the very depths of their being, change whole cultures, the direction of nations and the very flow of history.[28]

We have tried to use stories to demonstrate the case for reviewing our practice as preachers and have made suggestions for different ways of doing this. Underlying this lies a spirituality of being open to the challenge of what God may be saying to us. Linked to this is an attitude of being prepared to change as an essential aspect of the Christian faith.

The benefits we see of developing reflective practice as preachers are:
- It helps us to maintain freshness.
- It stimulates us to try new approaches.
- It demonstrates pastoral care for our congregations.
- It enables us to continue to be learners.
- It is a means of identifying and evaluating the influences on our preaching.
- It is rooted in the biblical tradition of wisdom.
- It draws on differing styles of learning from experience.
- It can utilize many different approaches, which are applicable to a whole range of people and their experiences.

We hope that by offering different strategies for action we have paid due heed to each preacher having a different story to tell and a different range of experiences. Our use of different approaches to learning from experience is designed to complement this. We ourselves have employed the strategies advocated and have found them helpful. The aim of this booklet is to help you to have additional resources with which to improve your preaching of God's Word. We would like to encourage you to try in your preaching ministry some of the approaches we have mentioned.

---

27 Leonora Tubbs Tisdale, *Preaching as Local Theology and Folk Art* (Minneapolis: Fortress Press, 1997) p 96.
28 Richard Holloway, *Limping Towards the Sunrise* (Edinburgh: Saint Andrew Press, 1996) p 130.

7
Appendix: Worksheets

In preaching...competence is necessary and to be toiled for.[29]

This appendix includes a number of practical suggestions, which might help you in your preaching. You will see that they are from a number of sources. One way to start would be to try the approach which seems to speak to you.

1. Preaching Forbears[30]

Think of the time before you began preaching. Whose preaching did you listen to? What was their influence on you both positive and negative? What are their influences on you now? Write the answers down on a side of A4 and share with a friend. What new things did you see?

2. Profiling

The following grid is taken from the Central Readers Council *Profiles* document.[31] The idea is that evidence can be collected and then the grid filled in by both indicating the evidence and then evaluating yourself by ticking the boxes on a scale of 1 to 6. 0 is not yet started, 6 is my specialist ministry.

Preaching	0	1	2	3	4	5	6	Evidence
The person needs to show how far they have an understanding of the following and/or how they have demonstrated this in sample sermons.								
Construction								
Content: theology								
Content: Making connections								
Content: relevance								
Types of sermon								
Different congregations								
Different occasions								
Visual aids								

This identifies a profile of your preaching. You can then discuss this with someone, maybe a peer, and plan further developments. Clearly the grid could be developed to cover different criteria.

---

29 Donald Coggan, *New Day for Preaching* (London: SPCK, 1987, 1996) p 24.
30 This exercise comes from D J Schlafer, *Your Way with God's Word* (Cambridge: Cowley Publications, 1995).
31 Central Readers Council, *Profiles: A Tool for the Review of Reader Ministry* (London: CRC, 1997).

3. Your Personal Preaching Story[32]

Some will have done a lifeline exercise looking at the path of your life. The same can be done on your preaching ministry. Construct a preaching line, or a path, or a diagrammatic representation of your life story in preaching. What have been the ups and downs? Where has the road turned? Have there been dark patches or light patches? What might have contributed to the highlights and the bad experiences? What do you learn from all this? Try writing it down and sharing with a friend. What did you learn after the sharing?

4. What is it Like to Be?

Fred Craddock suggests an exercise to make sermons connect.[33]
1. Write the above phrase on a piece of paper and then, thinking of different people in the congregation,
2. Write a brief concrete description of three people, such as 'single,' 'with young children,' 'doing well,' 'taking an exam,' 'retiring,' 'sick,' 'tired out.'
3. Spend 15 minutes freely writing down what you imagine it would be like to be that person.

The idea is to put yourself in the shoes of your congregation as a part of your preparation to preach. You should take a page and divide it up as below.

What is it like to be?
Person 1
Person 2
Person 3

5. Analysing a Sermon

Sermons come in many shapes and forms. There are many good things to affirm about preaching. There is also scope for improvement in much of our preaching. One way of doing this is to analyse our sermons and see how we could improve them.[34] The aim is to heighten awareness of some of the issues in preaching. This method asumes that you can access your sermon either in a text or on a tape and that the sermon has a certain amount of structure or linear argument in it.

Thomas Long says that there are two things a sermon always needs—a *focus* statement (What is the theme of the sermon?) and a *function* statement (What do you want people to do?). The structure of the sermon should be a sequence that develops these two points. This gives a simple approach for analysis.

---

32 This idea was developed by John Waller for a workshop at the GROW Swanwick Conference 2000.
33 F Craddock, *Preaching* (Nashville: Abingdon Press, 1985).
34 From Thomas Long, *The Witness of Preaching* (Louisville: Westminster/John Knox Press, 1989).

- Start with writing out the focus and function.
- Look at the themes in each paragraph.
- Look at the structure. See how this is developed in the sermon.
- Ask questions about how it fits together.

Using these points a piece of paper can be divided up as follows:

Focus: Function:			
Paragraph	Theme	Structure	Questions

Questions that could be asked are:

- How effective is the introduction?
- Are the points clear?
- Do they build on one another?
- Are the illustrations additive?
- What are the connecting methods?
- How effective is the conclusion?
- Is the Bible used appropriately?
- So what?

The re-examination of a sermon might show how next time it might be better and develop greater self-awareness in preparation.

In the table above the assumption is made that the text is on a separate piece of paper or on a tape. If this is so, number the paragraphs (in a different colour) as a way of identifying them. If the original was on a computer it becomes possible to put the text into a column, say two thirds of the page, and then write your comments in the white space.

6. Asking questions about your sermon

Sermons are live events. Sometimes, however, they lack this vitality. Alvin Rueter talks about the need to 'make homilies oral' and he identifies the following characteristics of spoken language.[35] It is:

---

35 A C Rueter, *Making Good Preaching Better* (Collegeville: The Liturgical Press, 1997).

- Immediate
- Direct
- In talking rhythm
- Lean
- Profuse

He suggests you look at a recent sermon and:

1. Rewrite any twisting sentences.
2. Ask: are the pronouns mostly first and second person? If not then rewrite them.
3. List any pompous expressions and change them.
4. List the passive verbs and see if any would be more immediate in the active.
5. See if you had any transitions that would help people to 'get back in.' If not where might some go?

7. Using the Bible in Preaching

We need from time to time to revisit our use of the Bible in preaching. Here is one way to do that. Take a sermon and make comments or notes on each paragraph asking the following sorts of questions.

1. What interpretive choices have I made? Could I have chosen differently?
2. What are the exegetical decisions behind what I say?
3. Are there any textual choices in what I said?
4. Have I been influenced by any point of doctrine in my interpretation?
5. Have historical issues influenced me in my interpretation?
6. With whom am I identifying in the passage ('goodies' and 'baddies')?
7. What issues am I really trying to address? In society? In the congregation?
8. How would it look if I had chosen different interpretive approaches? Would one of these have got my point over better?

When you have done this share it with a fellow preacher and see how you then develop your understanding of your use of Scripture.[36]

---

36 See also, R J Allen, *Contemporary Biblical Interpretation for Preaching* (Valley Forge: Judson Press, 1984).